t

LOOKING AT THE MECHANISMS AND PATTERNS OF EVOLUTION WITH GRAPHIC ORGANIZERS

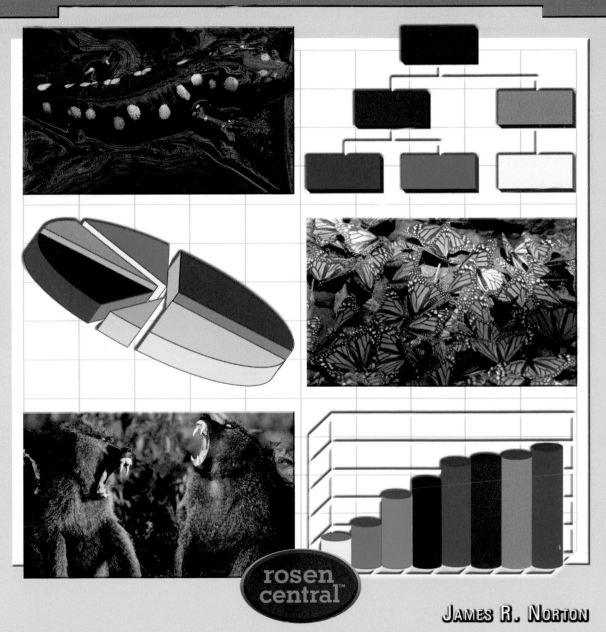

rosen
central ™

JAMES R. NORTON

The Rosen Publishing Group, Inc., New York

Published in 2006 by The Rosen Publishing Group, Inc.
29 East 21st Street, New York, NY 10010

First Edition

Library of Congress Cataloging-in-Publication Data

Norton, James R.
Looking at the mechanisms and patterns of evolution with graphic organizers/James R. Norton.—1st ed.
    p. cm.—(Using graphic organizers to study the living environment)
Includes bibliographical references.
ISBN 1-4042-0616-7 (lib. bdg.)
1. Evolution (Biology)—Juvenile literature. 2. Evolution (Biology)—Study and teaching (Elementary)—Graphic methods. 3. Graphic organizers—Juvenile literature.
I. Title. II. Series.
QH367.1.N67 2005
576.8—dc22

2005022041

Manufactured in the United States of America

On the cover: A tree chart *(top right)*, a pie chart *(middle left)*, and a bar chart *(bottom right)*.

CONTENTS

INTRODUCTION

Living things cover the earth. There is life at the bottom of the ocean, where animals use their own chemical illumination to light their way. There is life at the rocky, frigid tops of the world's tallest mountains. And there is life in the hottest of hot springs and in the coldest depths of the northern tundra.

No matter how alien or hostile the environment, living things have managed to identify their niche (area of specialty) and taken advantage of it. This is why some animals consume a single kind of food that other animals find indigestible. And it is why others, such as the incredibly versatile cockroach, will eat almost anything at all.

If you've ever wondered how animals and plants have so expertly managed to exploit Earth's natural resources—and one another—it helps to understand how species change over time. Scientists have come up with a theory that explains not only how Earth came to hold such a vast

Clockwise from left: models of various dinosaurs, which have long been extinct; a turtle, which is a living-fossil animal that has changed little over thousands of years; a stick insect, which has developed a defense by mimicking twigs; and a gorilla, which like other primates, including humans, has undergone dramatic changes over time.

variety of living things but also how these life-forms might continue to change over the years to come.

The theory of evolution helps us unravel some of the strangest questions of the natural world. How did bats develop sonar to "see" in the dark? How did octopuses develop eyes that are almost exactly like ours? Why do certain insects almost perfectly resemble leaves or twigs? But the biggest and most intriguing question that the theory of evolution answers is how humans came to think, walk, talk, and reason as we do.

Evolution is driven by a number of different mechanisms. Its effects become clear over time as species evolve, explode in numbers, or become extinct. Throughout this book, you'll see graphic organizers, or visual explainers, that will help explain the way evolution works and its long-term effects. These charts, graphs, and other kinds of graphic presentations illustrate concepts that support and explain how evolution works.

On the most simple level, evolution is the result of animals or plants reproducing and passing on their genes—or not reproducing and passing on their genes, due to pressure from the environment that kills them or otherwise prevents them from creating offspring.

Genes are the biological instructions that all living things, including people, carry within themselves. They determine what kinds of cells grow in our bodies, what we can safely eat, what temperatures we're comfortable with, what we're allergic to, what diseases we're vulnerable to, and a whole host of other attributes, or "traits," that can be passed on from parents to their offspring.

"Successful" animals and plants reproduce and pass on their genes and their traits. "Unsuccessful" animals and plants die before they get the chance. In this way, the environment—the weather, other animals, natural disasters—and luck determine who gets to live and reproduce and who dies without passing on their genetic instructions to another generation. This environmental pressure, which punishes animals and plants with certain traits while rewarding others, is called "natural selection."

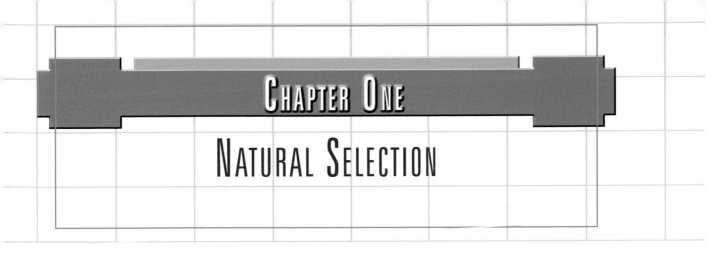

CHAPTER ONE

NATURAL SELECTION

In 1831, a twenty-two-year-old theology student named Charles Darwin (1809–1882) went on a five-year voyage aboard the HMS *Beagle*, a British naval survey ship. Darwin was on board as the ship's naturalist. It was his job to study the various plants and animals that the ship's crew would discover during their journey around the world. Darwin brought with him an insatiable curiosity and a willingness to always ask "why" and "how" about even seemingly obvious or simple parts of the natural world.

The discoveries that Darwin made on his voyage helped lay the groundwork for the modern theory of evolution, now well supported by many kinds of evidence. A rough version of the theory of evolution already existed when Darwin made his trip. But it wasn't until after Darwin's *On the Origin of Species* that the theory approached its modern shape and world recognition.

THE THEORY OF NATURAL SELECTION

According to biologist Ernst Mayr, Darwin's theory was a mix of five basic ideas. First, there is the nonconstancy of species. This is the idea that species change over time and that they are ever-changing groups of individuals, not fixed, unchanging forms.

The second idea is the descent of all life-forms from common ancestors. Darwin suggested that every modern species has its origins in an older, often extinct species from the past.

Third, there is the gradualness of evolution. Evolution does not happen overnight with sudden changes. For example, an animal does not go from having no eyes to fully developed eyes in one step. Evolution happens in little steps.

The fourth idea is the multiplication of species. Over time, species change and branch off, multiplying to fill different opportunities and niches provided by nature.

Finally, there is the idea of natural selection. Competition from other species, changes in environment, disease, and other factors put pressure on populations and help select for (or against) certain traits.

In *On the Origin of Species,* Darwin writes:

I am fully convinced that the species are not immutable; but that those belonging to what are called the same genera are lineal

E-CHART: EVIDENCE OF EVOLUTION

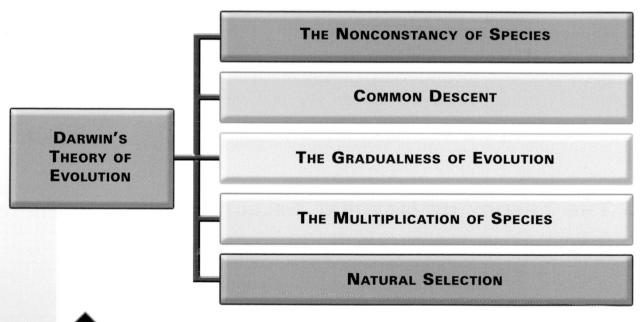

This graphic organizer is called an E-chart, because of its resemblance to the capital letter *E.* E-charts are useful for presenting a whole range of relationships between a main idea, which is placed on the left side, and supporting details, which go on the branches of the *E.* This E-chart lists the five basic ideas of Charles Darwin's theory of evolution.

descendants of some other and generally extinct species, in the same manner as the acknowledged varieties of any one species are the descendants of that species. Furthermore, I am convinced that Natural Selection has been the most important, but not the exclusive, means of modification.

Because of his groundbreaking research in evolutionary science, Charles Darwin is often referred to as the father of modern biology.

Natural selection was the revolutionary idea that Darwin stumbled upon in the Pacific Ocean's Galápagos Islands and put into words in *On the Origin of Species*. Natural selection suggests that different sorts of pressures, such as disease, changing habitats, predators, and competitors for food, weed out weaker members of a species. This pressure changes the overall makeup of the species' population, killing the less fit members while the more fit members live on to breed and pass along their genes.

THE ROLE OF GENES

Genes are the units within every living thing that act as the source code for life. They literally make us what we are, controlling the chemical processes that build new plants or animals from the moment they are conceived. Genes play a key role in evolution, which rewards helpful mutations in the genetic code of plants and animals. Mutations are copying errors made to the genetic material in the process of creating a new baby plant or animal.

These copying errors result in a change in the genetic code, and on rare occasions, alter the physical attributes of the mutated plants or animals. Sometimes these new attributes—such as longer,

A finch feeds on a rock in Santa Cruz, the Galápagos Islands, Ecuador. Thirteen of the fourteen species of birds that are recognized as Darwin's finches are found in the Galápagos. The other is on Cocos Island.

warmer hair; sharper teeth; or a more flexible tail—help the organism survive. If it survives and breeds, it can pass on its new genes to its offspring.

PATTERNS OF EVOLUTION

Although Darwin lacked our modern understanding of genes and biology, he was able to make observations in the Galápagos that helped him detect the patterns of evolution. Some of his most important observations were of the finches that lived on the islands.

Darwin identified thirteen species of the birds, but he was surprised because he knew of only one species of finch on the nearby continent of South America. Since the Galápagos are close to South America and no other large mass of land, the original island finch must have come from the continent.

The various species of island finches, Darwin noticed, differed from one another in beak shape. What's more, the beaks of the finches were shaped perfectly to take advantage of the food available on their islands. He concluded that after dispersing to the various island environments, the original finch species evolved over time because of the pressure of finding food. Finches were rewarded for having the right beak for the food at hand on their specific island. In other words, a single finch species flew out to the Galápagos and over time became many different species well adapted to take advantage of each of the unique island environments.

Today we call this sort of branching evolution adaptive radiation. Darwin learned that all populations consist of individuals, all

LINE GRAPH: DIRECTIONAL SELECTION

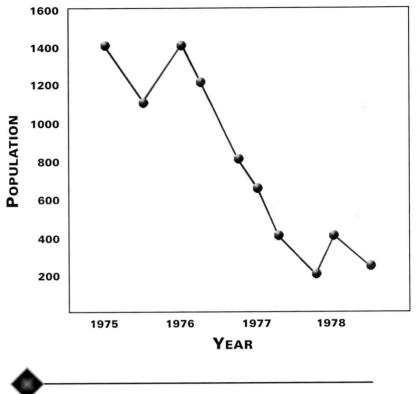

of which are at least slightly different from one another. Individuals that have a variation that gives them an advantage in surviving long enough to have offspring make their own traits more common as the population evolves. Darwin called this process descent with modification.

Scientists working in the Galápagos Islands in the 1970s made a new observation that supported and echoed Darwin's ideas. A drought on one of the islands had

Line graphs are good for showing trends. This line graph shows the steady decline in the population of a medium-sized ground finch in the Galápagos Islands between 1975 and 1978, a result of a drought that drastically reduced the seeds on which the finch fed. Two or more population counts were taken each year.

greatly cut down on a plant that produced small seeds. The seeds were the main food for a species of island finch.

Finches with larger, deeper beaks were able to break open the hulls of larger, tougher fruit in order to survive. Finches with small beaks died out in much larger numbers during the drought. As a result, the overall finch population still alive after the drought had larger and deeper beaks than the finch population before the drought. Baby finches after the drought, born to parents with larger and deeper beaks, tended to have larger and deeper beaks themselves.

THREE-COLUMN CHART: DIRECTIONAL SELECTION 2

	BEAK LENGTH	BEAK DEPTH
DEAD BIRDS	10.68 MM	9.42 MM
SURVIVORS	11.07 MM	9.96 MM

This chart compares the beak length and depth of the Galapagos finches that survived the mid-seventies drought with those of the dead birds.

LINE GRAPH: THOMAS MALTHUS AND POPULATION GROWTH

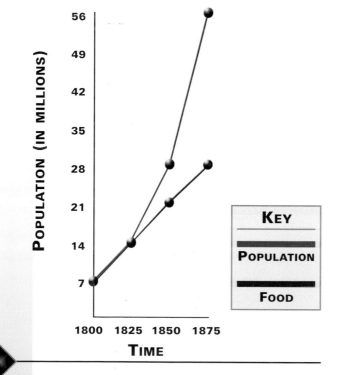

KEY

POPULATION

FOOD

This graph charts Thomas Malthus's theory that population increases at a faster rate than the supporting food supply.

The drought, therefore, acted to select for finches with bigger beaks, pushing the finch species in a new direction. The drought had acted as a pressure to reward the genes of the finches with bigger beaks.

Darwin's theory was also influenced by the theories of another British thinker, Thomas Malthus (1766–1834). Malthus wrote about how food tends to increase slowly while population explodes much more quickly. The resulting gap between food supply and population means that violent competition for food and famine are inevitable. The gap puts a pressure on the population, so that only the most fit individuals are able to eat and thus survive.

Although Malthus's theory on the principle of population does not accurately describe how food and population relate in the real world, it was clear enough to help Darwin understand the way environmental factors can shape a population, by killing its weakest members and eliminating their genes.

CHAPTER TWO

THE BIOLOGY OF EVOLUTION

All life goes back to chemical messages that living things carry within themselves. These messages, called genes, are the instruction booklets for building the next generation of plants or animals. Our genes govern what our children's hair and eye color will be, how tall they're likely to be, what genetic diseases they will be vulnerable to, and when their bodies are likely to shut down and start to die. Our parents' genes determined our physical makeup.

Our genetic instructions are encoded in something called DNA. DNA, which stands for deoxyribonucleic acid, is shaped like two twisted spiral staircases, a shape known as a double helix. The steps on the staircases are linked pairs of chemicals including adenine, guanine, thymine, and cytosine. The order of these stairs is a code that tells a newly forming plant or animal how to build itself.

CELL REPLICATION AND SPECIES SURVIVAL

Cells replicate through mitosis and meiosis. Mitosis, which takes place in the body's normal growth process, is the splitting of a cell into two identical cells. Meiosis, which is necessary for reproduction, results in four cells, each with half the genetic material of the parent cell. Errors in these copying processes usually have no effect, but sometimes they prove fatal. They can create harmful birth defects, harmless birth defects, or even useful adaptations that will increase the organism's chances of surviving in the world.

DNA Base Pairing

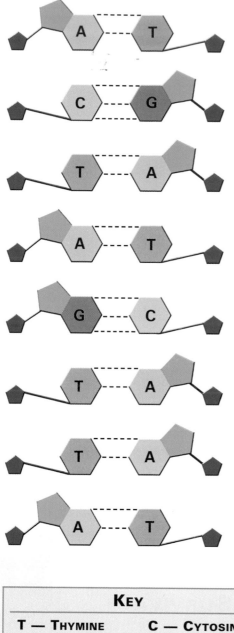

KEY	
T — THYMINE	C — CYTOSINE
A — ADENINE	G — GUANINE

The sample base pairing sequence in this diagram illustrates how the molecular bases of DNA strands (thymine, adenine, cytosine, and guanine) connect with one another via hydrogen bonds.

Although Darwin's theory did a lot to explain the diversity of the world's life-forms, it had an important flaw. It failed to explain how diverse, unusual individuals preserved their distinct genetic presence in the population after breeding.

In Darwin's day, the common understanding was that genes blend when plants or animals breed. After a few generations of breeding, therefore, every individual pretty much looks like every other individual—genes become very standardized "compromises" between different traits. No single mutant trait can exist very long before being blended back into the population as a whole.

MENDEL'S CONTRIBUTION TO EVOLUTIONARY THEORY

A monk named Gregor Mendel changed the way people looked at genes. Mendel lived in Moravia (the modern-day Czech Republic) from 1822 until 1884. Although he was not a professional scientist, he made discoveries that redefined the way the world looked at genes. He also helped to support Darwin's theory in the process.

Mendel's discoveries are crucial to Darwinian evolution. Under the old understanding of genetics, the "blending" system, all genes within a species become a single type of blended mix over just a few generations of breeding.

Diverse traits and potential for mutation are quickly lost because all the individuals within a species eventually have exactly the same genetic makeup.

TREE CHART: BLENDING AND MENDELIAN INHERITANCE

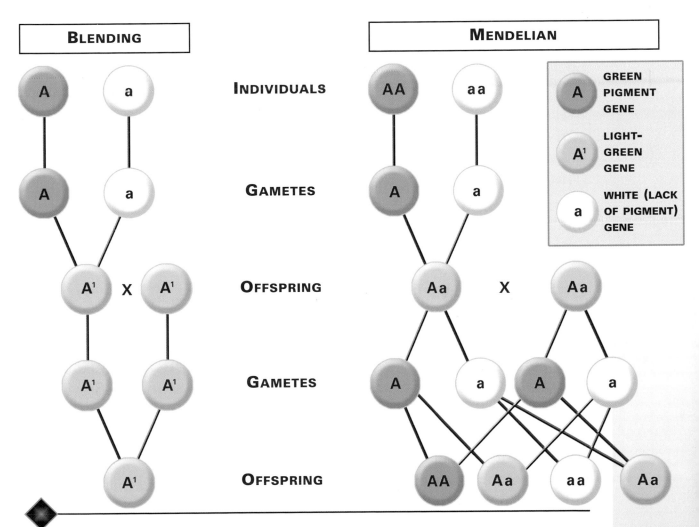

These tree charts compare the blending and Mendelian theories of inheritance, using the example of the cross-pollination between two pea plants; one producing green peas, and the other, white peas. Unlike in blending genetics where mixing the two plants produces a new light-green gene, Mendelian genetics hold that the new peas, though light-green in color, retain their green and white genes, and are capable of yielding white, green, and light-green peas.

Mendel tested this theory by breeding many generations of peas, crossing different varieties with one another and tracking how the different traits (such as color) came and went over the generations. It took him seven years, but Mendel was able to disprove the "gene blending" theory through careful work.

According to Mendel's experiments, genetic variations are preserved. Individuals retain unique genetic attributes after breeding, even if they are "recessive" and don't manifest themselves as visible traits. Even the extremely rare genetic types are preserved and passed down over time as members of the species mate. This makes it possible for newly evolved traits to become established within an existing population, instead of quickly becoming blended away over the course of a few generations. But under either system, if any particular type of life-form hopes to be successful in passing along its genes to future generations, it needs to live to be old enough to have offspring, and then have as many healthy offspring as possible.

SPECIES COMPETITION AND NATURAL SELECTION

There are a wide variety of strategies used by different species to pass along their genes to future generations. Humans, elephants, and pandas have only a few children, which they raise carefully, watching patiently until the children are fully able to take care of themselves. Others species, such as frogs, spew out tens of thousands of eggs, which they then abandon. The survival rate of the carefully reared offspring is much, much higher than the scattered eggs, which are gobbled down like candy by predators. But there are so many more eggs (and then, tadpoles, and then, frogs) that even with horrifying losses at the early stages, the frogs can do quite well in the long run. Every species has its own strategy for trying to raise as many healthy young ones as possible. Compare, for example, the coconut tree, which drops a few huge, well-protected nuts, with the dandelion, which scatters thousands of its seeds to the wind, borne aloft by tiny parachutes of fuzz.

In general, the urgent competition to raise healthy young and the natural-selection pressure of the environment make species stronger and stronger over time. But sometimes a population suffers a disaster, such as a flood, a sustained attack by human hunters, or a terrible disease. Its numbers fall drastically before rebounding, passing through a period biologists call a bottleneck.

COMPARE/CONTRAST WHEEL:
THE FIGHT FOR VIABLE OFFSPRING

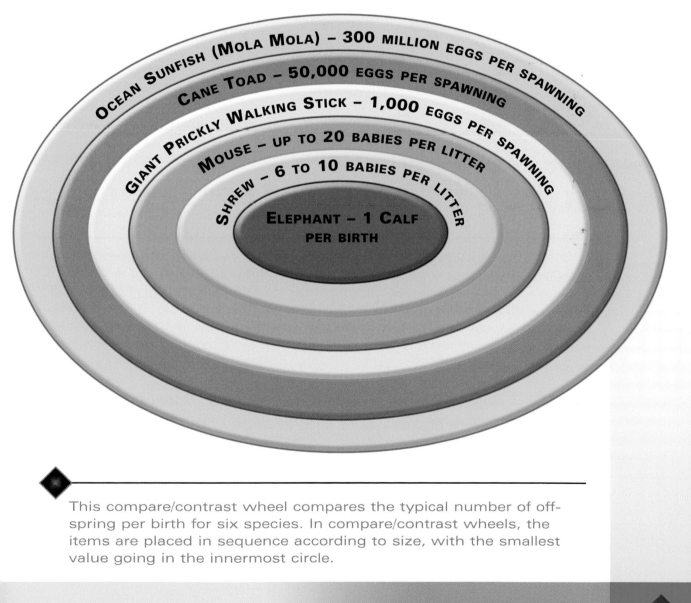

OCEAN SUNFISH (MOLA MOLA) – 300 MILLION EGGS PER SPAWNING

CANE TOAD – 50,000 EGGS PER SPAWNING

GIANT PRICKLY WALKING STICK – 1,000 EGGS PER SPAWNING

MOUSE – UP TO 20 BABIES PER LITTER

SHREW – 6 TO 10 BABIES PER LITTER

ELEPHANT – 1 CALF PER BIRTH

This compare/contrast wheel compares the typical number of offspring per birth for six species. In compare/contrast wheels, the items are placed in sequence according to size, with the smallest value going in the innermost circle.

SEQUENCE CHART: BOTTLENECK PRESSURE

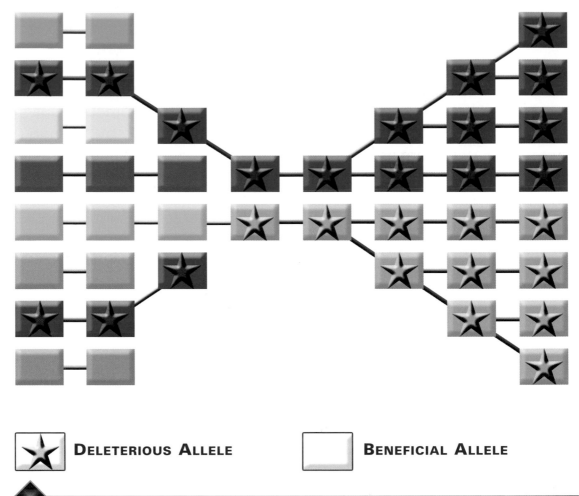

⭐ **DELETERIOUS ALLELE**   ☐ **BENEFICIAL ALLELE**

Sequence charts are useful for showing the chain of events that flows from one or more events. This chart illustrates bottleneck pressure. When a population is decimated, the amount of genetic variation available within the population plunges as well. The surviving population may have a comparatively high number of harmful alleles. As the population recovers from the bottleneck, the proportional increase in these alleles can weaken the fitness of the whole population.

Imagine a population of cheetahs living in Africa. Typically, the fastest cheetahs survive and are best able to cope with their environment and catch fast prey such as antelope. But then a terrible drought strikes the area, lasting for generations. The cheetahs best able to conserve and go without water are the survivors, regardless of whether they can run quickly or not.

Eventually, water returns to the area, and the cheetah population rebounds. But after passing through the bottleneck of the drought, the cheetah population has changed. Many fast cheetahs have been killed off, and the water-efficient cheetahs are now the dominant sort of cheetah in the population, thus shifting the nature of the population.

Over many generations, the speed of cheetahs may again be the main trait shaping the population, but for now, water-efficiency is far more common than it usually is and high speed is less common than it was, possibly hurting the long-term health of the species overall.

Thus, a bottleneck can greatly harm a species by overinflating the presence of a particular adaptation. Or it can harm a species by concentrating a previously rare genetic flaw (such as a nasty genetic disease) and turning it from a rare fluke into a common affliction. Therefore, evolutionary pressure is not always a positive thing. Natural selection does not always select traits that help a species in the long term.

The cheetah is the world's fastest land animal. Unlike other members of the cat family, it relies on its speed, rather than stealth or pack tactics, to hunt its prey.

It should also be noted that while natural selection is one of the most important pressures that causes evolutionary change, it is not the only pressure at work. When populations are small, they are vulnerable to something called genetic drift. Key traits can be lost with relatively few mutation errors or chance deaths of certain individuals within a small population. In a large population, locally lost genes tend to be replaced by gene flow from other parts of the population. But in a small population, genetic drift can change the nature of a whole species.

CHAPTER THREE

EVOLUTIONARY FORCES

The evolution of a species does not exist in a vacuum. A change in a species has an impact on every other species sharing its ecosystem. When a seabird becomes better at diving, for example, it might catch more of a certain sort of fish. Suddenly, the other predators of that fish feel the pressure to find other ways of keeping themselves fed. And the fish itself has more pressure to live at greater depths, in order to avoid being turned into a diving bird's dinner.

ADAPTATION TO CHANGES IN THE ECOSYSTEM

One classic example of this sort of interplay between environment and evolution has been studied in England since the middle of the nineteenth century. The peppered moth lived on trees throughout England, using its black-and-white splotched coloring to hide among light-colored lichens on tree trunks. Its predators could rarely spot the moth as it hid among the lichens.

But a strange thing happened as England became increasingly polluted during the coal-driven Industrial Revolution. Lichens began dying off, and in industrial parts of England (such as Manchester and Liverpool), the tree trunks became dark in color. The light-colored moths started getting picked off the dark trees by predators, such as birds. Dark-colored moths—very rare before pollution—became increasingly common in polluted areas.

Over time, as pollution spread, the moths with genes that caused them to be dark-colored became more numerous, and the peppered moth became increasingly an all-black species.

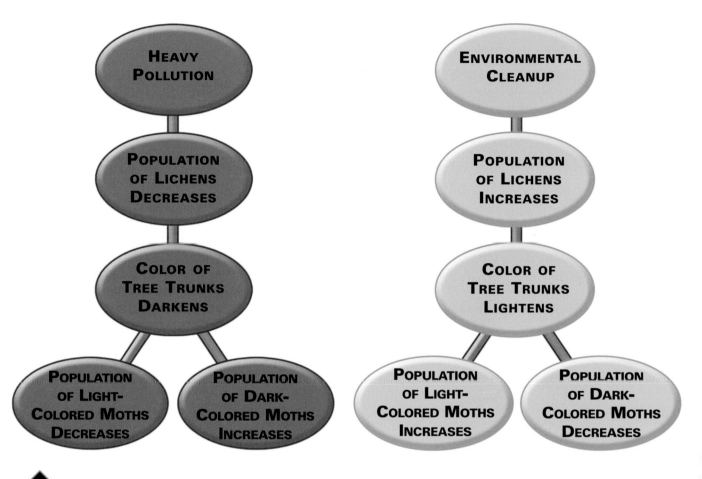

These side-by-side tree charts illustrate the sequence of effects many theorize heavy pollution had on lichens, tree trunks, and light- and dark-colored moths in Great Britain during the Industrial Revolution, and, second, the reversal of these effects during a period of antipollution measures during the 1960s and 1970s.

Then, in the 1960s and 1970s, Britain began cleaning up its act. Old coal-driven factories were shut down or modernized to reduce pollution. Lichens began returning to the trees, and the light-shaded version of the peppered moth staged an incredible comeback across the country, as it found more and more lichens in which to hide from its predators.

Sometimes, it's not just the prey species that evolves in order to stay ahead of the game. Sometimes prey species evolve a defense, and their predators, generations later, come up with a countermeasure to render that defense useless.

Such is the story with the hatchet fish, which dwells in a dark and murky part of the ocean. In this part of the water, light is scarce, and fish can barely be spotted against the faint daylight that glimmers down to its extreme depths. But that slight visual cue is enough for the silent hunters of the deep, which lock onto silhouettes of fish like the hatchet fish and then strike with lethal force.

The hatchet fish, over time, evolved cells on its belly to mimic the daylight overhead. This made it extremely hard to pick out the hatchet fish against the few rays of the sun penetrating to its level of the ocean. But then, over time, larger fish began to evolve specialized eyes capable of telling the difference between faint natural sunlight and the artificial light of the hatchet fish. Suddenly, the hatchet fish's defense was useless. Will the hatchet fish evolve a still better type of false light, or another kind of defense altogether? It's quite possible, but only time will tell.

The story is the same around the world in many different ecosystems. As a prey species gets faster, predator species speed up. As the prey learns to hide in the grass, predators start to detect them by sound or scent. As a prey species develops venom, its predators adapt by eating clay—

CYCLE CHART: ADAPTATION AND COUNTER-ADAPTATION

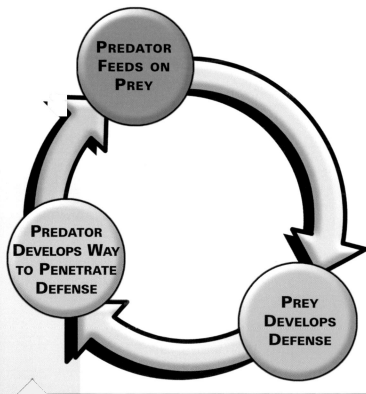

This chart shows the cycle of adaptation and counter-adaptation that is typical among predators and prey. This cycle develops over generations.

a natural way to neutralize many of the natural world's nastiest toxins.

As Darwin predicted, useful adaptations are typically retained and provoke counter-adaptations as predators evolve. After all, if the predators didn't evolve, they couldn't ensure constant access to their prey and exploit new weaknesses among the species upon which they prey.

MIMICRY

In the struggle to avoid being eaten—a very important contest that takes place every day, in a thousand different ecosystems— a bewildering array of evolutionary tactics have arisen. One of the

Monarch butterflies are also known as milkweed butterflies because its young (larvae) feed only on the milkweed plant. Adult females also lay their eggs on the plant.

most striking is the tactic of mimicry. The classic example—which has been disputed in recent years—involves the monarch and viceroy butteflies. According to this theory, the monarch is fortunate enough to evolve natural toxins that make it disgusting to predators. A bird might eat one monarch, but it's unlikely to eat another after its first nauseating experience. The monarch, therefore, has picked up an evolutionary advantage that it capitalizes upon with distinctive coloring that warns predators to back off!

It is an advantage that another butterfly, the viceroy, has taken advantage of. The coloring of the viceroy, over many generations, has come to resemble that of the monarch's. A predator that has tasted the disgusting monarch will also avoid the nontoxic and comparatively tasty viceroys, warned off by the viceroys' similar coloration. Originally, viceroys didn't look much like monarchs, but there was an evolutionary advantage to looking more and more

THREE-COLUMN CHART: MIMICRY

MIMIC	MODEL	BENEFIT
VICEROY BUTTERFLY	MONARCH BUTTERFLY	PREDATORS MISTAKE THE MIMIC AS BEING POISONOUS.
STICK INSECT	TWIG	PREDATORS PERCEIVE THE INSECT AS A TWIG.
WEEVIL	FLESH FLY	PREDATORS MISTAKE THE SLOW-FLYING WEEVIL AS BEING SPEEDY.
SCORPION FISH	SEA PLANTS	PREY DO NOT SEE THE MOTIONLESS FISH AGAINST THE PLANT UNTIL IT'S TOO LATE.
AEGERIA MOTH	YELLOW JACKET WASP	PREDATORS MISTAKE THE MOTH AS CAPABLE OF STINGING.

This three-column chart gives fives examples of mimicry, describing the advantage gained by each mimic species.

like their toxic cousins. Therefore, viceroys that looked even a little like monarchs were more likely to survive and therefore pass on their genes. Random mutations and natural selection led to viceroys looking more and more like monarchs, until the two species became almost identical.

Some animals accomplish similar goals by mimicking inedible objects. The stick insect, for example, looks like an inedible twig and will hang out nearly motionless in order to complete the illusion. It's a disguise that works, and so the genes keep getting passed on from one generation to the next.

THREATS TO THE ECOSYSTEM

Sometimes, the evolution of a particular trait will move a species from being a competitor with a few other animals to being a general threat to everything that shares its ecosystem and a source of natural selective pressure for most of the species with which it comes into contact. The cane toad of Australia is extremely toxic.

BAR GRAPH: SELECTIVE PRESSURE

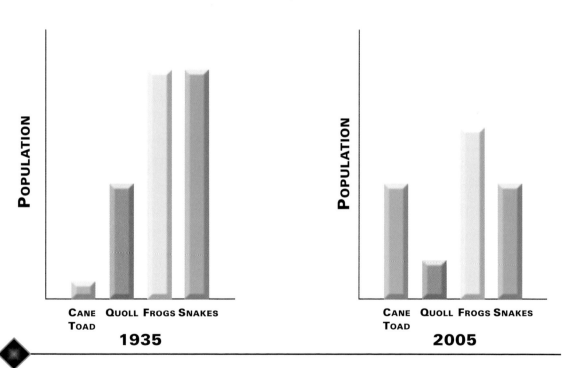

Bar graphs are useful for comparing and contrasting the values of two or more things or of the same thing at different times. These bar charts roughly show the ratio of the invasive cane toad to three other Australian species in 1935 and 2005. A comparison of the two charts reveals how the growth of the cane toad's population resulted in a decline in the population of quolls, frogs, and snakes.

Cane toads are prolific breeders, the female laying anywhere from 4,000 to 36,000 eggs at a time and twice each year. The eggs and the tadpoles are toxic to many animals, which increases their chances of achieving maturity.

Imported by humans to control pests destroying sugar cane crops, the toad quickly went native and bred rapidly in the Australian wilderness. It eats just about everything smaller than itself, sucking up insects like a vacuum cleaner, leaving little for other predators to eat. Almost anything bigger than the cane toad will eat it and then immediately die from its incredibly strong toxins. Its appearance in the ecosystem of northeastern Australia has been catastrophic, driving some native marsupial species toward extinction and serving as a factor causing natural selection for most of the species that cross its path.

As destructive as the cane toad has been to the Australian wildlife, already some kinds of birds have figured out how to flip the toad over and eat its considerably less-poisonous belly. And if its numbers stay high enough and its presence stays strong enough, it is likely other Australian animals will eventually evolve natural antidotes to the toad's poison so that they can tap into the toad as a food resource.

The complicated evolutionary dance between predator, prey, and environment has been going on nearly since the beginning of life on Earth, almost 4 billion years ago. Although evolutionary theory helps us understand many aspects of it, biologists are still working to figure out precisely how plants and animals alter one another over time.

CHAPTER FOUR
PATTERNS OF EVOLUTION AND EXTINCTION

A radical change in environment can have a radical impact on the world's life-forms. When a large meteorite strikes Earth, for example, many things happen. The impact creates a massive earthquake. It clouds the atmosphere with dust that blocks the sun. It creates massive wildfires, which also fill the atmosphere with pollutants like soot and dust. It creates chemicals called nitrogen oxides, which also enter the atmosphere. The dust blocks the sun for months or even years, contributing to a global cooling and changing the world's climate. And the nitrogen oxides create acid rain, making the oceans more acidic.

These kinds of changes can be devastating to species perfectly adapted to a different sort of environment—a warmer Earth, or a less acidic ocean, for example. A new ice age—or dramatic global warming—could kill off hundreds or thousands of species over a very short period of time. In fact, over history, there have been many such mass extinctions.

A single catastrophic event, such as a meteor strike, can have a domino effect on Earth's species. If the strike wipes out most of the small fish in a particular river, for example, all the larger predators that eat that fish are in danger of dying off as well. At the same time, a species competing with the small fish for resources might suddenly come into its own and explode in numbers, taking advantage of the new environment.

TIMELINE CHART: MASS EXTINCTIONS

440 MILLION YEARS AGO	**ORDOVICIAN-SILURIAN EXTINCTION** **LIKELY CAUSE: DROP IN SEA LEVEL AS GLACIERS FORMED, THEN RISE IN SEA LEVEL AS THEY MELTED.** **SPECIES WIPED OUT: 25 PERCENT OF MARINE FAMILIES**
365 MILLION YEARS AGO	**LATE DEVONIAN EXTINCTION** **LIKELY CAUSE: UNKNOWN** **SPECIES WIPED OUT: 22 PERCENT OF MARINE FAMILIES; LITTLE KNOWN ABOUT LAND LIFE-FORMS**
250 MILLION YEARS AGO	**PERMIAN-TRIASSIC EXTINCTION** **LIKELY CAUSE: COMET OR ASTEROID IMPACT** **SPECIES WIPED OUT: 95 PERCENT OF ALL SPECIES**
200 MILLION YEARS AGO	**END TRIASSIC EXTINCTION** **LIKELY CAUSE: MASSIVE FLOODS OF LAVA AND GLOBAL WARMING** **SPECIES WIPED OUT: 22 PERCENT OF MARINE FAMILIES; VERTEBRATE DEATHS UNCLEAR**
65 MILLION YEARS AGO	**CRETACEOUS-TERTIARY EXTINCTION** **LIKELY CAUSE: IMPACT OF SEVERAL-MILE-WIDE ASTEROID** **SPECIES WIPED OUT: 16 PERCENT OF MARINE FAMILIES; 18 PERCENT OF LAND VERTEBRATE FAMILIES INCLUDING DINOSAURS**

A timeline chart is a table that lists a number of events in chronological order. This timeline lists history's five major mass extinctions, giving the likely cause of each as well as the life-forms that were wiped out.

MASS EXTINCTION

A wide range of global natural events can lead to mass extinctions. A change in sea level is thought to have caused the Late Cambrian extinction 500 million years ago. The extinction wiped out many of the world's brachiopods (shelled invertebrates with a fleshy stalk which anchors them to the seafloor), conodonts (eel-like vertebrates), and trilobites (ancient arthropods, somewhat like modern insects).

The Late Devonian extinction, which wiped out many marine invertebrates 365 million years ago, is believed to have been caused by global cooling. And the Cretaceous-Tertiary extinction, which wiped out the dinosaurs 65 million years ago, is thought to have been caused by a meteorite impact, although other theories include volcanic activity or even cosmic radiation.

Mass extinctions can have a very broad and deep impact on life, affecting and reshaping life at most of the lower steps of the evolutionary hierarchy that separates broad classes of animals and plants from much more specific groupings such as species.

This illustration shows brachiosaurs in a swamp. Brachiosaurs were large plant-eating dinosaurs that lived in North America during the late Jurassic period, around 145 million years ago.

RADIATIVE ADAPTATION

Most patterns of evolution are less dramatic than the mass extinctions, which are relatively infrequent from a historical perspective. Branching evolution—also known as radiative adaptation—is a pattern that biologists have observed ever since Darwin studied finches in the Galápagos.

The Laupala cricket is just one of the most recently observed examples of radiative adaptation. American scientists studied thirty-eight species of this cricket, which originally came from an unknown continental mainland as a single species.

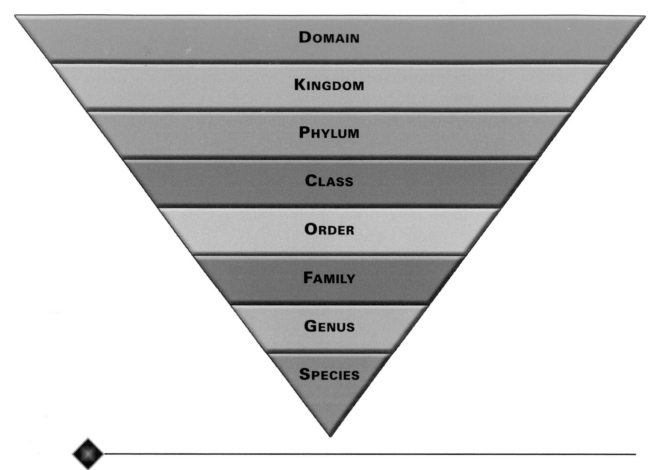

DOMAIN

KINGDOM

PHYLUM

CLASS

ORDER

FAMILY

GENUS

SPECIES

In order to describe the relationship between different sorts of living things, scientists have devised a hierarchy of life-forms. This can be effectively illustrated on an inverted triangle. The level at the top of the hierarchy is the broadest and most inclusive. The level at the bottom of the hierarchy is the most specific—an individual species.

When the crickets arrived on the Hawaiian Islands, they found many different kind of environments waiting for them. Each island is its own ecosystem, subdivided into many small ecological niches. Over time, the Laupala crickets specialized in different niches, branching off from a single ancestor species to thirty-eight better-adapted new species. All of this happened in a relatively short period of time. New Laupala species evolved at the rate of about four per million years, according to the scientists, making them one of the fastest-evolving invertebrates. Evolving differences in the crickets' complicated mating songs sped the separation of

Maps are typically used to show locations. They are also useful for illustrating other things, such as population density and distribution. This map shows the number of Laupala cricket species found on each of the Hawaiian Islands. The sole species on Lanai may now be extinct.

cricket species, say the scientists. Because crickets will mate only with crickets singing the right kind of song and because songs can change easily without other factors (such as competition for a unique ecosystem niche or a food source), the original Laupala crickets quickly split apart into many new species, each with its own kind of courtship song.

LIVING-FOSSIL SPECIES

On the other end of the speed spectrum are living-fossil species such as lungfish, ginkgo trees, platypuses, and horseshoe crabs.

LINE GRAPH: RATES OF EVOLUTIONARY CHANGE FOR THE LUNGFISH

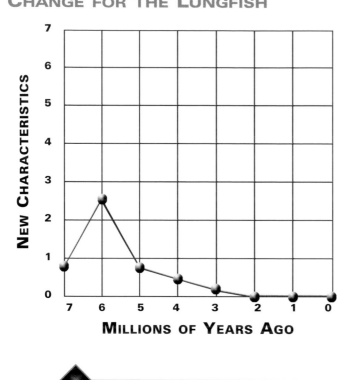

Some species are known as living fossils because of their unchanged resemblance to creatures living hundreds of millions of years ago. Over time, these species become optimally adapted to a stable environment, and their rate of evolutionary change drops to almost nothing. The rate of change in lungfish species has slowed to a halt over time. This line graph charts the number of new characteristics gained by lungfish over the last 7 million years. Note that it has remained virtually unchanged in the last 3 million years.

Living-fossil species have not changed in any significant way for tens of millions of years, and their rate of evolution has seemingly slowed down to a complete halt because they have so perfectly adapted to their ecological niche. Living fossils like the lungfish don't resemble any other living species—all their close relatives died off in the distant past. Due to a fluke of luck or a great adaptive fit to a specific environment, the living fossils have managed to hang on to their old-fashioned genes.

Therefore, there is no given single "speed" at which life evolves. The speed of evolution can be greatly increased when a relatively small population is subject to rapidly changing environmental conditions. Certain conditions, such as those experienced by the Laupala cricket, offer much opportunity, incentive, and means for change. Other conditions, such as those experienced by the many living fossils, lead to slow or almost totally nonexistent evolutionary progress.

CHAPTER FIVE

EVOLUTION AND HUMANKIND

The evolution of humans is one of science's most controversial stories. While there are still debates about the specific timeline of ancestral species that eventually evolved into the modern human, there is a generally agreed-upon

TIME-ORDER CHART: THE RISE OF HUMANKIND

MILLIONS OF YEARS AGO

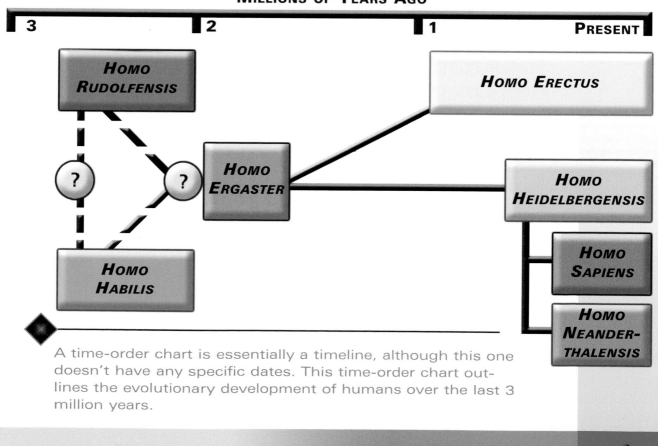

A time-order chart is essentially a timeline, although this one doesn't have any specific dates. This time-order chart outlines the evolutionary development of humans over the last 3 million years.

Fossil records provide convincing evidence that humans evolved from four-legged apelike animals. Over time, the four-legged ancestors underwent skeletal modifications that began when they were adapting to life in trees. Eventually they became capable of walking upright on two legs. Further modifications led to greater dexterity and manipulative skills, improved vision, a reduced reliance on smell, and a larger and more complex brain. Modern humans emerged around 40,000 years ago. Since then, human evolution has been largely cultural.

progression from more apelike species such as *Homo habilis* (Latin for "handy man") up to modern humans, *Homo sapiens*.

Cultural and religious traditions have often drawn a line between humanity and the animal world, but the fossil and genetic record says otherwise. Although humans are among the most adaptive and certainly the most intelligent creatures on Earth, we trace our roots back to creatures of humbler origins, who most likely lived on the great grassy plains of Africa.

In Darwin's day, the idea that humans directly evolved from animals was particularly explosive. Darwin himself was cautious when first writing about his conclusion about man's descent. But his theory of common descent, which says that all living organisms are descended from common ancestors, made the conclusion about humankind's primate origins unavoidable.

Anatomical evidence supports Darwin's claim. Humans are very similar physically to the African apes, particularly the chimpanzee. Although humans have a few unique details (such as the size of our forebrains and the mobility of our thumbs), we otherwise very closely resemble our primate cousins.

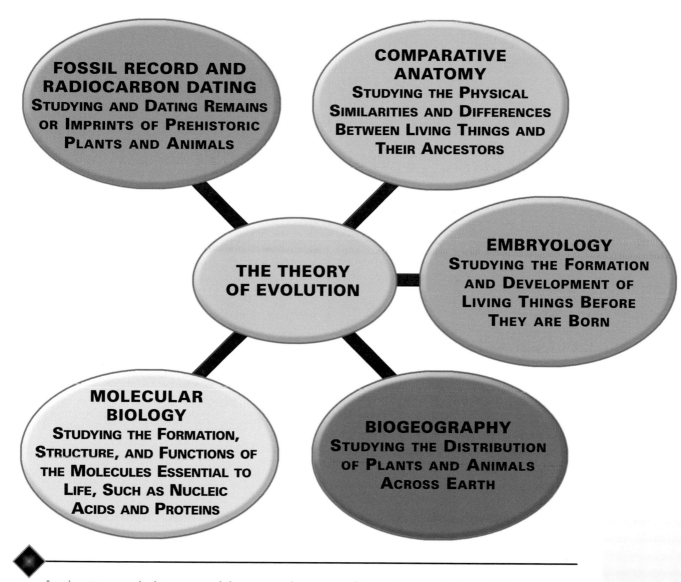

A cluster web is a graphic organizer used to show relationships between concepts. The main concept is placed in the center and related details are place around it, connected by lines. This cluster web lists and explains the five main fields of study that support the theory of evolution.

Fossil evidence supports the idea that humans broke off from the chimpanzee and developed in their own different but related evolutionary direction. Many fossils of humanlike ancestors have been unearthed, and they've helped us fill in the timeline that leads up to modern humans. It's a timeline that still needs more data. The next generation of paleontologists is unlikely to run out of work.

Enhanced daytime vision, including depth and color perception, was one of the most significant trends in the evolution of humans and other primates.

Molecular biology also supports the descent of humans from apes. Human molecules are more similar to those of chimpanzees than those of other organisms. Biologists have even found that the similarity is so close that certain proteins—such as hemoglobin, which moves oxygen and carbon dioxide around in the bloodstream—are virtually identical between humans and chimpanzees. This doesn't mean, however, that humanity isn't unique. It's a remarkable species, and its sophisticated tool use, huge brain, and long period of child rearing, among other things, set it apart.

CONVERGENT EVOLUTION

Some of humanity's most impressive anatomical attributes don't set it apart from other creatures, however. They illustrate one of evolution's most amazing patterns, that of convergent evolution. One such attribute is the human eye. It's able to focus on things very close to itself (like the text you're reading right now) or things far away on the horizon. It can see a vast spectrum of colors. It can pick up on movement, particularly in its peripheral (side) fields of vision. It's a complex organ, involving a combination of elements such as a lens, an optic nerve, an iris, and a retina.

How did the eye evolve? We can look to lower life-forms such as shrimp and flatworms for at least one explanation. Even a very primitive eye (such as a patch of light-detecting cells) can provide an evolutionary advantage to a creature living deep in the ocean. With time, those cells can grow slightly in complexity and—like the eye of the flatworm—begin to detect movement as well as light. In fact, every one of the eye's many complicated aspects helps improve the odds of survival. As the eye gets more and more complex, it picks up additional attributes. It can see farther and farther, pick out finer and finer details, and track movement more precisely. Thus, incremental improvements can lead, over millions of years, to the evolution of something as complicated as the human eye.

The octopus eye is remarkably similar in appearance and function to the human eye. This shared feature, despite the vast differences in the two species, is an example of convergent evolution.

While it's amazing that the human eye exists, it's perhaps even more amazing that another eye exists that's very similar to it—the octopus eye. But humans and octopuses don't share any recent ancestors. You have to go way back in time before you find shared ancestry between the two species. Both evolved similar eyes independently because in both cases, a sensitive and multipurpose eye offered a real survival advantage.

When two creatures evolve similar features independently to do similar jobs, it's called convergent evolution. The same sort of evolutionary forces pushed dolphins (which are mammals) to evolve stabilizing dorsal fins very similar to those of sharks (which are fish and, therefore, only very distantly related to dolphins).

Convergent evolution is present all over the world. Different species that descended in radically different ways find similar solutions to similar problems. Fish in the Arctic, for example, were found in the 1960s to have adapted a special trait that allows them to live in cold water. They evolved molecules called glycoproteins, which act like antifreeze, circulating in the blood of the fish and

Compare/Contrast Chart: Dolphins Versus Sharks

DIFFERENCES   **SIMILARITIES**   **DIFFERENCES**

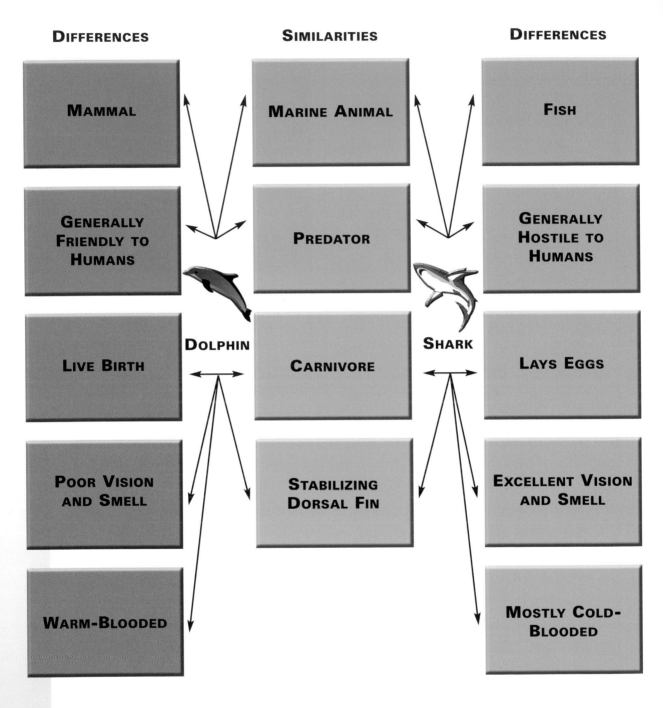

MAMMAL	MARINE ANIMAL	FISH
GENERALLY FRIENDLY TO HUMANS	PREDATOR	GENERALLY HOSTILE TO HUMANS
LIVE BIRTH	CARNIVORE	LAYS EGGS
POOR VISION AND SMELL	STABILIZING DORSAL FIN	EXCELLENT VISION AND SMELL
WARM-BLOODED		MOSTLY COLD-BLOODED

DOLPHIN   SHARK

This compare/contrast chart outlines some of the similarities and differences between dolphins and sharks. Though the two species seem similar in appearance, they are two vastly different types of animals.

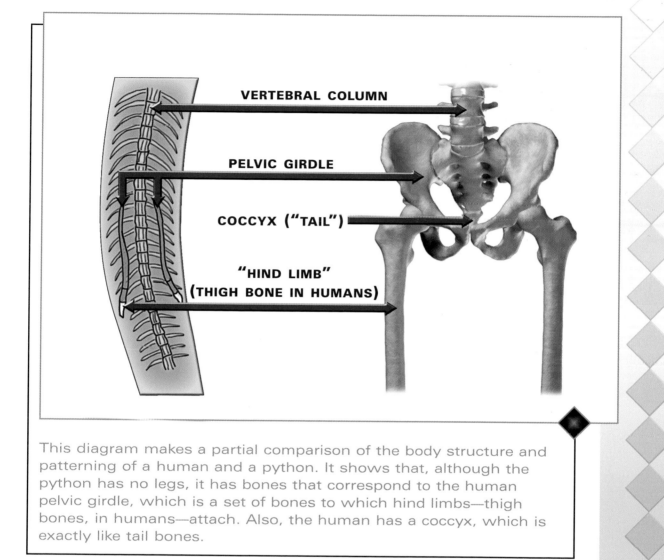

VERTEBRAL COLUMN

PELVIC GIRDLE

COCCYX ("TAIL")

"HIND LIMB"
(THIGH BONE IN HUMANS)

This diagram makes a partial comparison of the body structure and patterning of a human and a python. It shows that, although the python has no legs, it has bones that correspond to the human pelvic girdle, which is a set of bones to which hind limbs—thigh bones, in humans—attach. Also, the human has a coccyx, which is exactly like tail bones.

keeping it from freezing. This is an amazing adaptation. But what is more amazing still is that fish at the other side of the world, in the Antarctic, were found to have evolved similar antifreeze proteins.

Faced with the same problem, two different kinds of fish evolved similar solutions, despite being at opposite ends of Earth and totally unrelated to one another. Like the octopus and the human evolving incredibly similar eyes, this is an example of life's ability to come up with effective solutions to challenging natural problems.

This photograph of a bat with its wings spread shows the similarities of its limbs to human limbs.

ADAPTIVE MODIFICATION

Another of evolution's quirks is how similar structures in related creatures can be used for radically different things. If you look at a human's arm, it is very well adapted to our day-to-day activities. Our fingers are strong but nimble, and they are good for tool use. Our arms can lift relatively heavy loads and are in a good proportion to our legs and the rest of our body. But the same basic bones of the human arm have been radically repurposed by other mammals in a process known as adaptive modification.

A bat's wing, for example, has the same bones as the human arm does—a radius, an ulna, a humerus, and carpal bones. But for the bat, the carpals—which would be fingers for human beings—have become long, delicate structures that support their wings. For a whale, the carpal bones have become squat and strong as they are used to sustain a flipper. Manual dexterity is not important to whales, which live in a radically different world than we do.

Although not all evolutionary processes lead to useful adaptations like a bat's wing or a human's fingers, evolution has created the sprawling variety of life that we encounter every day, wherever we may live. From the spider's web to the anteater's sticky tongue, evolution provides answers to many of nature's mysteries. And for that reason, among others, evolution is a force worth understanding.

GLOSSARY

adaptation Any aspect of a living thing believed to add to its overall fitness.

allele One member of a pair or series of genes that occupy a specific position on a certain chromosome.

biogeography The analysis of the spatial distribution of life-forms.

convergent evolution The evolution of two species in a manner that produces similar features through the influence of natural selection, not common ancestry.

Cretaceous-Tertiary extinction Probably the most famous mass extinction in history, it wiped out the dinosaurs, pterosaurs (flying reptiles), and many types of fish, plankton, and other species 65 million years ago.

DNA (deoxyribonucleic acid) Any of the nucleic acids that are usually the molecular basis of heredity. The acids are constructed of a double helix held together by hydrogen bonds.

ecosystem A community of organisms and its environment functioning as a unit.

embryology The study of the formation and early development of animals before they are born.

evolution The process by which the living world has developed.

extinction In biology, the end of a species or group of species. It is estimated that 99.9 percent of all species that have ever lived are now extinct.

gene A sequence of nucleotides in DNA or RNA (ribonucleic acid) that controls the transmission and expression of one or more traits.

genetic drift A mechanism of evolution that acts with natural selection to change a species over time. It stems from the role of random sampling in the production of offspring. Drift works most strongly in small populations.

Late Cambrian extinction Mass extinction that occurred 500 million years ago, wiping out trilobites, conodonts, and brachiopods. Although the cause of the extinction is unclear, a change in sea level—and thus, habitat—is suspected.

Late Devonian extinction Mass extinction that occurred 365 million years ago, wiping out as many of 70 percent of all species. Its cause is unknown. Marine species, including brachiopods, ammonites, and agnathan and placoderm fish suffered the hardest hit.

living fossil A species surviving into the present day more than 50 million years after its relatives became extinct.

mass extinction A period in time when a large number of species die out.

meiosis A cellular process that forms the basis for sexual reproduction. Most animals and plants use meiosis to produce gametes, which fuse to form zygotes, which develop into new organisms.

mitosis The process of chromosome segregation and nuclear division that assures that each daughter nucleus receives a complete copy of the organism's genome.

mutation An inheritable change in genetic material. It's most commonly caused by errors during cell division.

natural selection A process by which individuals of greater fitness survive and their advantageous traits are perpetuated in the overall population.

population A group of organisms of the same species in a specific ecosystem.

radiative adaptation The divergence, through evolution, of a single original species into different environmental niches.

recessive gene The allele of a pair less likely to be expressed in an organism's phenotype than the other member of the pair.

ribonucleic acid (RNA) Any of the nucleic acids that contain ribose and uracil and control cellular chemical activities.

species A group of organisms that are capable of producing viable offspring.

theory A generally accepted broad explanation supported by evidence.

theory of common descent The idea that all living things started from one life-form and evolved in many different directions to adapt to many different environments.

For More Information

Department of Manuscripts
Cambridge University Library
West Road Cambridge
CB3 9DR
England
(01223) 333000
e-mail: library@lib.cam.ac.uk
Web site: http://www.lib.cam.ac.uk/MSS/Darwin.html

University of California Museum of Paleontology
1101 Valley Life Sciences Building
Berkeley, CA 94720-4780
(510) 642-1821
Web site: http://www.ucmp.berkeley.edu

WEB SITES

Due to the changing nature of Internet links, the Rosen
Publishing Group, Inc., has developed an online list of Web sites
related to the subject of this book. This site is updated regularly.
Please use this link to access the list:

http://www.rosenlinks.com/ugosle/mpgo

FOR FURTHER READING

Lawson, Kristan. *Darwin and Evolution for Kids: His Life and Ideas with 21 Activities* (For Kids Series). Chicago, IL: Chicago Review Press, 2003.

Liebes, Sidney, Elisabet Sahtouris, and Brian Swimme. *A Walk Through Time: From Stardust to Us: The Evolution of Life on Earth*. New York, NY: John Wiley & Sons, 1998.

Stein, Sara. *The Evolution Book*. New York, NY: Workman Publishing, 1986.

Westberg Peters, Lisa, and Lauren Stringer. *Our Family Tree: An Evolutionary Story*. New York, NY: Harcourt Children's Books, 2003.

BIBLIOGRAPHY

Brandon, Robert N. *Adaptation and Environment*. Princeton, NJ: Princeton University Press, 1990.

Darwin, Charles. *The Origin of Species*. New York, NY: Random House, 1993.

Dawkins, Richard. *River Out of Eden: A Darwinian View of Life*. New York, NY: Basic Books, 1995.

Eldredge, Niles, ed. *The Natural History Reader in Evolution*. New York, NY: Columbia University Press, 1987.

Lewin, Roger. *Patterns in Evolution*. New York, NY: Scientific American Library, 1999.

Mayr, Ernst. *What Evolution Is*. New York, NY: Basic Books, 2001.

Ridley, Mark. *Evolution*. Malden, MA: Blackwell Publishing, 1993.

INDEX

ABOUT THE AUTHOR

James Norton is a research director for a radio show and an editor. His father, Robert Norton, an amateur geologist and fossil collector, spurred his interest in evolution. He lives in Brooklyn, New York.

PHOTO CREDITS

Cover, pp. 1, 5 © Royalty-Free/Nova Development Corporation; pp. 4–5 © Jonathan Blair/Corbis; pp. 8, 11, 12 , 14, 15, 17, 18, 21, 22, 24, 25, 28, 30, 31, 32, 33, 35, 38, 39 courtesy of Nelson Sá; p. 9 © Michael Nicholson/Corbis; p. 10 © Tim Graham/Getty Images; p. 19 © Gallo Images/Corbis; p. 23 © Richard Cummins/Corbis; p. 26 © Galen Rowell/Corbis; p. 29 © Jim Zuckerman/Corbis; p. 34 © James W. Porter/Corbis; p. 36 © Getty Images; p. 37 © Stephen Frink/Corbis; p. 40 © Gary Braasch/Corbis.

Designer: Nelson Sá; Editor: Wayne Anderson; Photo Researcher: Nelson Sá